kid$ense
Presents

The Dazzling Dollar Dude

Making $ense of Your Ċents

Mary Becker

Illustrations by Tim Williams

This book is dedicated to Millie, my mother-in-law, with heartfelt gratitude for raising a remarkable son who became my husband.

—Mary

BOOKLOGIX˙
Alpharetta, GA

Second Edition

ISBN: 978-1-61005-759-2 - Paperback
ISBN: 978-1-6653-0546-4 - Hardcover
eISBN: 978-1-61005-760-8 - ePub
eISBN: 978-1-61005-761-5 - Mobi

Library of Congress Control Number: 2016902391

10 9 8 7 6 5 4 3   1 1 1 1 2 2

♾ This paper meets the requirements of ANSI/NISO Z39.48-1992 (Permanence of Paper)

Cover art and illustrations by Tim Williams

INTRODUCTION

FOR TEACHERS AND PARENTS

The Dazzling Dollar Dude teaches just how easy it can be for a child to become his or her own superhero by having a simple money plan. Our impatient "me-centered" society emphasizes that one can have whatever one wants immediately, robbing many individuals the reward of delayed gratification and the chance to learn how to be a savvy shopper who can control impulse buying. Once money is spent, it is gone! Perhaps the greatest loss is the opportunity to experience the joy of giving to others or the pride that comes with saving and earning something on one's own. So how can children gain wisdom and make sense of their cents? This story will help children learn in a *Keep It Super Simple* (K.I.S.S.) way by following the secret code of three letters: G.S.S. Developing solid money management habits and strong financial decision-making skills can be one of the most challenging practices to master. Mr. 3-D will help your child learn these crucial life skills in a fun way. Happy reading!

The I. O. Lots family lives on a street,
With neighbors you'd think that you never could meet.
Miss Ima Spendthrift is really a shopper;
Lack of cash in her pocket never does stop her.
The Ben Shopping family is nearly as bad;
They never keep track of the money they've had.
And right next door lives Miss Penny Snatcher;
She charges so fast that banks never catch her!

When the family came home from Moe Frugal's store,
They saw their best friend standing by his front door.
The debt monster also was there on this day;
Mr. I. M. Broke was being taken away!
It was obvious by all the bumps on his head,
He'd hit his debt ceiling and could not get ahead.
It was just as plain as the nose on his face;
He'd hit his debt ceiling and could not erase
All the bills that he owed for things he had bought.
Oh, how I. M. Broke wished that he had been taught
How to manage and save the money he'd earned.
It was one of those things that he never had learned.
It was then I. O. Lots knew just what to do;
He needed to find a plan and he knew
Just the right person to call on the phone.
He just could not figure this out on his own.

"I am calling Moe Frugal;
    There's more to the plan
About handling money;
    He's a very smart man."

The phone went "ring-ring," and Moe said, "Hello."
Mr. Lots was upset; he wished he did know
More about how folks should handle expense.
He needed a plan that was good common sense!
Moe Frugal was happy to call his best friend.
3-D was the person that he'd recommend.
"I know just the person that you need to meet;
He's a real superhero with a sidekick that's sweet.
I'll call him right now to come over and teach you;
I know he's the one that you need to speak to!"

"Ring-ring" went the phone, and 3-D said, "Hello . . .
I am ready to help anyone that you know."
"Go right to their house," said the little old man;
"This family needs help, and I know that you can."
So 3-D got his gear and loaded his car.
The trip wouldn't take long; the house wasn't far.

He knocked on their door and said, "How do you do?
Moe Frugal did call me and did ask me to
Come right on over and show you my plan.
I know I can help your family, young man."

"But I am surprised at how you are dressed.
Like, where is your cape? I'm just not impressed."

"I know my appearance may be a surprise,
But some superheroes do wear a disguise.
They look like real people, and you'd never guess
That they are true heroes by the way that they dress.
For genuine heroes are really quite brave,
And they do make wise choices, and many do save
People or buildings or somebody's pet.
My job is to help people stay out of debt.
But if you want a hero 'out-of-the-blue,'
I'll do something super I don't always do.
In a 'poof' of an instant I'll change how I'm dressed
And you'll see my cape and the crest on my chest."

"How awesome!" the brother did say with a grin;
"Please come meet my family. Oh please, do come in!"

"But what is your name?"
    Asked the curious brother.
"Yes, what is your name?"
    Asked the dad and the mother.

"**DAZZLING DOLLAR DUDE**
    is my given name:
That's **3-D** for short . . .
    still means the same."

"That must be why you are dressed all in dollars;
It shows everyone you're the wisest of scholars."

"I've done my research on money; it's true;
And now I am ready to share it with you.
All you need is the plan I will show you today.
Just listen and learn and don't go astray.
You'll need to remember to follow that plan.
And here's the best news: I know that you can!"

The man dressed in dollars went to his car
And picked up three boxes that looked quite bizarre.
He carefully stacked them on top of his head.
The letters **G**, **S**, and **S** were easily read.

He carried them into the house right away,
Set each on the floor and then he did say,
"Listen quite closely, and I'll show to you
All of my secrets . . . some old and some new."
"Who is that butterfly that sits on your head?
She is so pretty," the young sister said.
"Yes, my sidekick's a beauty and so very sweet;
Ms. Two-Cents-Worth's the one I'd like you to meet."

"It's a pleasure to meet you," she said with a smile.
"I add my 'two cents worth' every once in a while.
If you look very closely while my wings do not flutter,
You will see two wise words that make debt monsters stutter.
For the homophone pair that you see here today
Reminds folks to make 'sense of their cents,' as we say . . .
Please follow the plan that 3-D will display;
It is sure to keep debt monsters far, far away!"

"Now that is exciting!" the father did say;
"So please do get started and show us today."
"Which is the first box that you'll open now?"
Asked the littlest sister as the cat said, "Meow."
"That's a very good question," 3-D said with a grin,
And he thought very hard as he did scratch his chin.

Ms. Two-Cents-Worth smiled and then she did say,
"You should open the box by 3-D right away."
Then she flapped her wings and a key did appear.
She had said her two-cents-worth; she was very sincere.
"We will start out our plan with the box that's marked **G**;
Please unlock that box now using this key."
And she handed the key to the wide-smiling brother;
"This is exciting!" said the dad and the mother.

The brother removed the key from his fist;
He opened the box with a twist of his wrist.
And "POOF!" . . . what they saw was quite a surprise,
For 3-D had changed from his normal disguise!

And from under the lid, there did arise
Many things floating in front of their eyes.
There was a quarter, a dime, a nickel, a penny;
Next were smiles and kind words . . .
    Of those there were plenty.

And all of the family was very surprised
By the things that were floating in front of their eyes.
"But we don't understand it; how can it be?
It is not just money that all of us see."

"Well, let me explain," said 3-D with a smile.
"The **G** is for **GIVING**, which is so worthwhile.
A kind word, a good deed, or maybe some clothing;
Now plan to give money without others knowing!
There are churches, food pantries, overseas missions,
The Red Cross, service clubs, even soup kitchens.
There are so many places where you could donate,
And the amazing thing is that you will feel great.
For one of the greatest secrets of living
Is the joy that you'll feel when you are giving.
The money you give to others, you see,
Is just the beginning in the plan of the three."

"So let's go to box two with the big letter **S**
And see if you know or if you can guess."
"That **S** must be special for something," said Dad.
"I know that the **S** just cannot be bad."
"At first," said 3-D, "you just might be mad,
But after some thinking I think you'll be glad.
The **S** is for **SAVING**; I know you're upset,
But remember the plan is to stay out of debt!"
The dad said to 3-D, "You can see I am stunned,
But if this is needed, then we'll start a fund.
We will always be careful to set money apart
To save for the future; now that would be smart.
We'll save some money just as you say;
In fact, we can start to save money today!"

"And now," said 3-D, "with no further ado,
Ms. Two-Cents-Worth will open the last box for you."
"Oh yes!" cried the siblings. "Please open it now!"
"As you wish, my dear friends," he said with a bow.

When the lid was removed, it was such a surprise!
They couldn't believe what they saw with their eyes.
Each single person saw something quite rare;
Each saw what they wanted floating in air.

The mom saw a coat she had wanted to buy;
The dad really wanted an airplane to fly.
The siblings were all jumping up so excited;
They could hardly believe all the toys that were sighted.
There were games and toy cars; there were dolls and toy dishes.
There were all kinds of things that would fill all their wishes.

"Do you know," asked 3-D, "what the last **S** stands for?
This **S** is for **SPENDING** for things at the store."
"Oh wow!" they exclaimed. "Are you sure that is true?
We thought our shopping and spending were through."

"Oh no," said 3-D. "You just need to know
Whatever you're buying so you have your dough!
Make a list of the things that your heart desires,
And when you have money in hand, be a buyer.
But always remember unless you can say,
'I have cash in my pocket; I'm paying today.'
Unless you can say that is totally true,
Go back to your list or maybe step two.
So please do get started and write down your plan.
It's fun and it's easy, and I know that you can!"

"How can we thank you for what you have done?
This plan makes good sense and should be such fun
To fix our own boxes marked **G**, **S**, and **S**;
We will **GIVE**, **SAVE** . . . then **SPEND**, and we'll do our best
To follow this easy and fun money plan.
It makes 'sense of our cents'; now we know that we can!"

There was a loud "POOF," and what did they see?
Why they saw the original Mr. 3-D . . .
As he and his sidekick packed up the car.
Their trip home wouldn't take long; their house wasn't far.
Now, please go get started with your own money plan.
You'll have fun, and it's easy, and we know that you can!

IDEAS FOR DISCUSSING

THE DAZZLING DOLLAR DUDE & "PACKING YOUR MONEY PLAN"

Remember in the story when Ms. Two-Cents-Worth handed the key to the brother? He unlocked the boxes and learned the secrets to being money wise. Let's talk about how you can be money wise too.

1. The first box is marked with **G** and stands for **GIVING**. There are many ways to give money to others. Who would you like to help? Where would you like to give? Why? How would you do it?
2. The next box is marked **S** and is for **SAVING**. Is there a special reason that you want to save your money? Is there something that really costs a lot of money that you are hoping to pay for or buy?
3. The last box in the group is marked **S** for **SPENDING**. Some people like to buy tickets to see a movie. Some people like to buy candy or toys. Is there any special way that you like to spend your money? What do you like to do that costs money?
4. What would you do if you went shopping and you wanted to buy something but didn't have enough money to buy it right now? Would you ask someone for the money? Would you take the money you needed out of your savings? Would you wait until you had more money in your spending box? What would you do?
5. Why should **GIVING** and **SAVING** come before **SPENDING**? How can you best remember this?
6. Do you earn money? Do you receive money for birthdays or holidays? Do you have a plan for what to do with your money or do you just spend it and wonder why it disappears so quickly? Why not do what the children in *The Dazzling Dollar Dude* did:

Thanks to 3-D and what he has done!
This plan makes good sense and should be such fun.
Now fix your own boxes marked G, S, and S;
And **GIVE**, **SAVE**, then **SPEND**, and you'll do your best
To follow this easy and fun money plan.
It makes 'sense of your cents'; now you know that you can!

Say yes to G.S.S.!

Grade Level Dolch Sight Word List Found In
The Dazzling Dollar Dude

Pre-primer				
a	down	in	not	to
and	find	is	one	two
away	for	it	red	up
big	go	little	said	we
blue	help	make	see	where
can	here	me	the	you
come	I	my	three	

Primer				
all	have	pretty	want	was
am	he	saw	was	well
are	like	say	well	went
at	must	she	went	what
be	new	so	what	who
but	no	that	who	with
came	now	there	will	yes
did	on	they	with	
do	our	this	yes	
get	out	too	this	
good	please	under	want	

Grade One				
an	every	his	old	thank
after	fly	how	once	them
an	from	just	open	then
as	give	know	over	think
ask	had	let	some	were
by	her	may	stop	when
could	him	of	take	

Grade Two				
always	call	many	us	would
always	does	read	very	write
been	don't	right	which	your
best	fast	their	why	
buy	first	those	wish	

Grade Two				
far	far	keep	never	start
about	got	kind	own	today
done	if	long	show	

Glossary

appearance: the way a person looks

bizarre: different, unusual, or odd; not what is normal

common sense: good choices that are made about everyday things

crest: a decoration or a symbol that means something

dazzling: amazing

debt: something that is owed to someone else

debt ceiling: when a person owes the most money that can be owed and cannot make the amount larger

desires: wishes

disguise: costume used to hide the way one looks

donate: to give away

dough: another word for money or cash

expense: the cost of having to buy something

frugal: careful with money

gear: things needed for a job or a special reason

homophone: two words that sound alike but are spelled differently and mean different things

instant: a very short amount of time

rare: not found very often

recommend: suggest

research: to study something very carefully

scholars: people who know a lot

sidekick: a close friend that helps

sincere: true

snatcher: someone who takes or grabs things quickly

spendthrift: someone who spends money without thinking

stunned: surprised

two-cents-worth: what a person thinks about something

Homophones Found In
THE DAZZLING DOLLAR DUDE

In *The Dazzling Dollar Dude*, Ms. Two-Cents-Worth had the words sense and cents on her wings. These two words are homophones. Homophones are words that sound the same but are spelled differently and mean different things. The words below in **BOLD, CAPITAL LETTERS** are used in *The Dazzling Dollar Dude*. The word(s) following the first word is/are its homophone(s). Do you know what each of the words mean? Can you spell each word correctly? There are thousands of homophones; can you think of some that are not on this list?

MEET/MEAT	**DO**/DUE/DEW	**READ**/RED
RIGHT/WRITE	**KNOW**/NO	**ADD**/AD
SO/SEW	**SENSE**/CENTS	**WHICH**/WITCH
THEIR/THERE/THEY'RE	**I'LL**/AISLE	**PAIR**/PEAR/PARE
BY/BUY/BYE	**I**/EYE	**HERE**/HEAR
ALL/AWL	**YOU**/EWE	**WE**/WEE
NOT/KNOT	**NEED**/KNEAD	**OUR**/HOUR
PLAIN/PLANE	**BUT**/BUTT	**GREAT**/GRATE
FOR/FOUR	**REAL**/REEL	**ADO**/ADIEU
OWED/ODE	**WOULD**/WOOD	**DOUGH**/DOE
ONE/WON	**WHERE**/WEAR/WARE	**BOW**/BOUGH
TO/TOO/TWO	**BE**/BEE	**AIR**/ERR
KNEW/NEW	**WAY**/WEIGH	
MORE/MOORE	**SEE**/SEA	
RING/WRING	**YOU'LL**/YULE	

JUST FOR FUN!

Below are thirty-seven Dolch sight words that are nouns. A noun is a person, place, or thing. The words below are hidden in the illustrations of *The Dazzling Dollar Dude*. How many can you find? Can you find all thirty-seven?

apple	door	Santa Claus
baby	father	sheep
ball	feet	shoe
box	flower	sister
boy	girl	street
brother	grass	table
car	hand	window
cat	head	
chair	home	
chicken	horse	
Christmas	mother	
coat	lamp	
cow	nest	
dog	picture	
doll	robin	

Tim Williams

About the Author

In fifth grade English class, Mary (Leary) Becker discovered her love of writing; that was the same year she discovered how fun it can be to spend money! Many years and purchases later, those two interests now combine in the entertaining and educational story of the I. O. Lots family. The author's hope is that *The Dazzling Dollar Dude* will lead families to great discussions about how to be wise stewards with their finances. Mary is presently living happily-ever-after with her high school sweetheart/husband in a storybook cottage, which includes a revolving door that is always open to their seven children, their children's spouses, and grandchildren.

For more information or other books by

Mary Becker,

please visit

MaryBeckerBooks.com

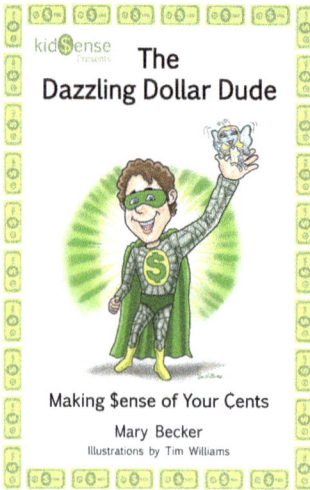

The
Dazzling Dollar Dude

Making $ense of Your Çents

Mary Becker
Illustrations by Tim Williams

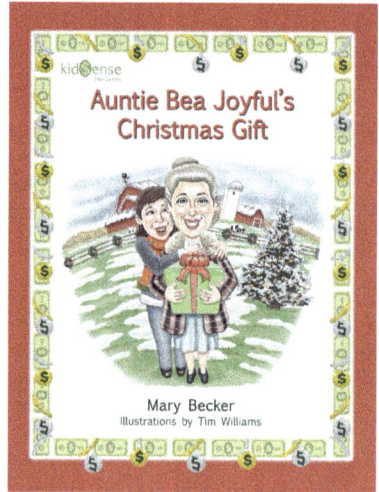

Auntie Bea Joyful's
Christmas Gift

Mary Becker
Illustrations by Tim Williams

You can also follow us on

Mary Becker Author

Thank you for reading my book.
Please consider sharing it with friends or family
and leaving a review online. Your feedback and
support are very much appreciated.

.

www.ingramcontent.com/pod-product-compliance
Lightning Source LLC
Chambersburg PA
CBHW071523210326

41597CB00018B/2867